How to Write a Book Report

by Cecilia Minden
and Kate Roth

CHERRY LAKE PUBLISHING · ANN ARBOR, MICHIGAN

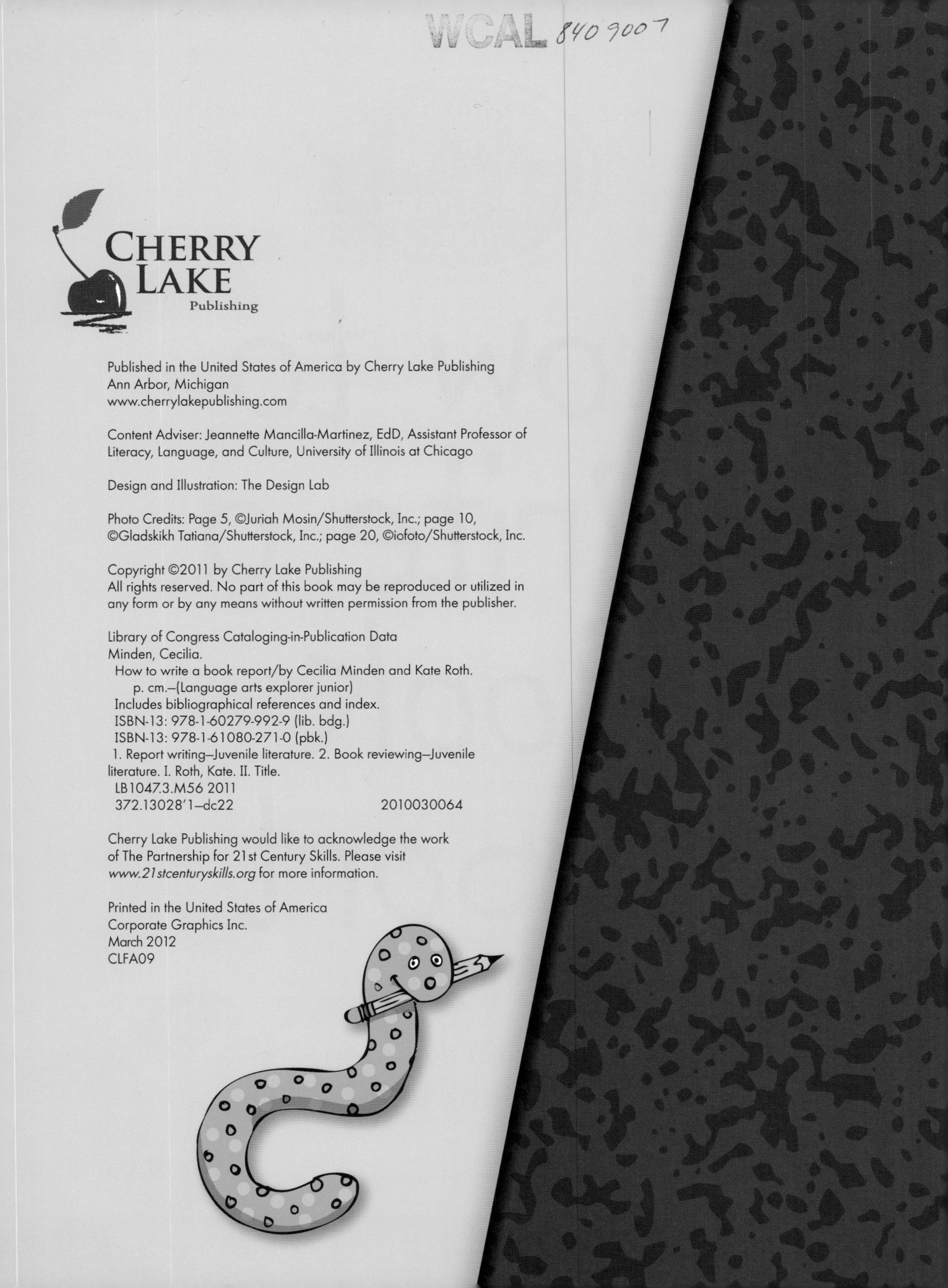

CHERRY LAKE Publishing

Published in the United States of America by Cherry Lake Publishing
Ann Arbor, Michigan
www.cherrylakepublishing.com

Content Adviser: Jeannette Mancilla-Martinez, EdD, Assistant Professor of Literacy, Language, and Culture, University of Illinois at Chicago

Design and Illustration: The Design Lab

Photo Credits: Page 5, ©Juriah Mosin/Shutterstock, Inc.; page 10, ©Gladskikh Tatiana/Shutterstock, Inc.; page 20, ©iofoto/Shutterstock, Inc.

Library of Congress Cataloging-in-Publication Data
Minden, Cecilia.
How to write a book report/by Cecilia Minden and Kate Roth.
p. cm.—(Language arts explorer junior)
Includes bibliographical references and index.
ISBN-13: 978-1-60279-992-9 (lib. bdg.)
ISBN-13: 978-1-61080-271-0 (pbk.)
1. Report writing—Juvenile literature. 2. Book reviewing—Juvenile literature. I. Roth, Kate. II. Title.
LB1047.3.M56 2011
372.13028'1—dc22 2010030064

Cherry Lake Publishing would like to acknowledge the work of The Partnership for 21st Century Skills. Please visit *www.21stcenturyskills.org* for more information.

Printed in the United States of America
Corporate Graphics Inc.
March 2012
CLFA09

Table of Contents

CHAPTER ONE

What a Good Book!

There are many kinds of books. Some are **fiction** books. The events and **characters** in these books are not real. Writers make them up using their imaginations. There are also **nonfiction** books. These books are about real people and events. A **biography** is an example of nonfiction.

Sometimes, teachers ask students to read books and write reports. A **book report** is a way to tell others about a book you have read. Book reports have many parts. They explain what the book is about. They also include your **opinion** of the book. Let's work on writing a book report!

Writing great book reports takes practice.

CHAPTER TWO

Parts of a Book Report

Your book report should include the title and author of the book. Is there an **illustrator**? Include this person, too.

Reports on fiction books should describe the **setting**, characters, and **plot**. The setting is where and when the story takes place.

Characters are usually the people or animals in the book. The plot is what happens in the book. There often is a problem and **solution**.

Nonfiction book reports are a bit different. They describe the book's subject. The subject is the person or thing that is written about in a book. What's the subject of a book about the sun? The sun! The book report also includes facts from the book.

Make a Chart

You've read your book. Now you need to organize your thoughts. A chart can help you do this. Look at the chart on page 9. It shows one way to map out the parts of a fiction book report. Now make a chart for your book.

HERE'S WHAT YOU'LL NEED:

- The book
- Notebook paper
- Ruler
- Pencil

INSTRUCTIONS:

1. Write your name and the date in the upper right corner of a sheet of paper.
2. Use a ruler to help you make the six boxes.
3. Do you see how the boxes in the chart on page 9 are labeled? Label your chart in the same way. Each box is for a different idea.
4. Fill in the boxes of your chart using information from your book. Leave the "My Opinion:" box blank for now.

Sample Book Report Chart

Name: Maria Day
Date: 3/19/2012

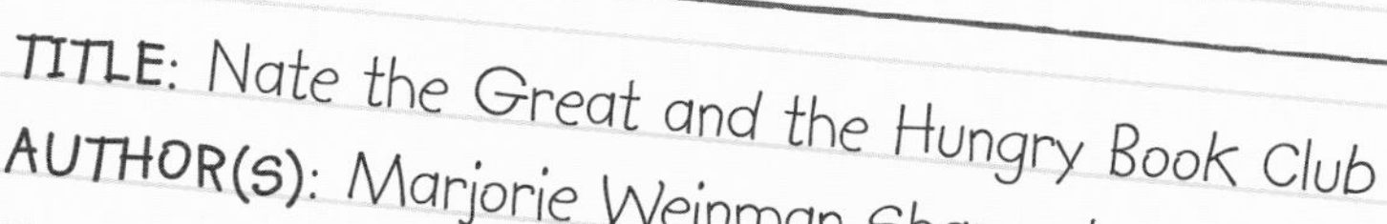

TITLE: Nate the Great and the Hungry Book Club
AUTHOR(S): Marjorie Weinman Sharmat and Mitchell Sharmat
ILLUSTRATOR: Jody Wheeler

CHARACTERS:

- Nate the Great
- Rosamond and her cats, the Hexes
- Sludge
- Annie and her dog

PLOT:

Beginning: Rosamond's book pages are missing.
Middle: Rosamond asks Nate to solve the mystery.
End: Nate solves the mystery.

SETTING:

- Rosamond's house (her kitchen)
- The school book sale

PROBLEM AND SOLUTION:

Book pages are ripped or missing. Nate finds out a cat is to blame.

MY OPINION:

CHAPTER THREE

What Do You Think?

It's okay if you didn't like a book. Be able to explain why.

Have you ever read a book report? Did it help you decide if you wanted to read the book? Your opinion of a book is important.

Share your ideas. Others will read your book report. It will help them decide if they would also like to read the book.

Opinions

Go back to the chart you started earlier. It is time to fill in the "My Opinion" box.

INSTRUCTIONS:

1. Ask yourself these questions:
   - Which characters did you like or not like? Why?
   - What was the best part of the book?
   - Are there pictures? Do they add to the story? How?
   - Should others read this book? Why?
   - Does this book remind you of another book you've read? Why?
2. Fill in the "MY OPINION:" box of your chart. Be sure to explain your opinions. Use information from the book to support and back up your ideas.

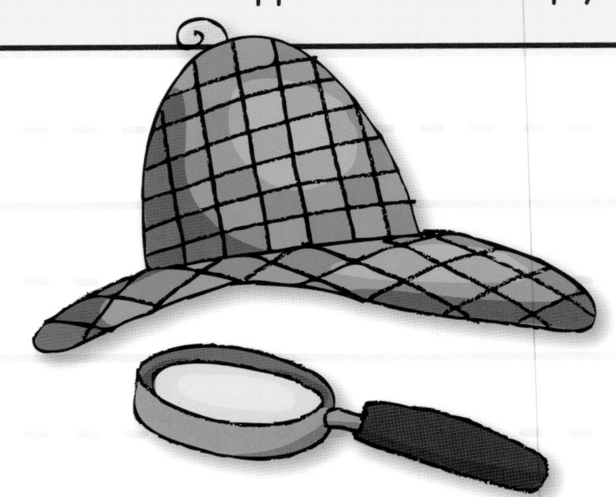

Sample Book Report Chart

Name: Maria Day
Date: 3/19/2012

TITLE: Nate the Great and the Hungry Book Club
AUTHOR(S): Marjorie Weinman Sharmat and Mitchell Sharmat
ILLUSTRATOR: Jody Wheeler

CHARACTERS:	**PLOT:**
• Nate the Great • Rosamond and her cats, the Hexes • Sludge • Annie and her dog	Beginning: Rosamond's book pages are missing. Middle: Rosamond asks Nate to solve the mystery. End: Nate solves the mystery.
SETTING: • Rosamond's house (her kitchen) • The school book sale	**PROBLEM AND SOLUTION:** Book pages are ripped or missing. Nate finds out a cat is to blame.

MY OPINION: I liked this book. I love to solve mysteries. I thought the characters were funny. The drawings helped me picture the action. I also liked trying to figure out the mystery before Nate.

CHAPTER FOUR

Nonfiction

Nonfiction book reports are written in a different way. You report on the facts you read in the book. You will also report on the setup of the book.

Nonfiction Chart

HERE'S WHAT YOU'LL NEED:

- The book
- Notebook paper
- Ruler
- Pencil

INSTRUCTIONS:

1. Write your name and the date in the upper right corner of a sheet of paper.
2. Use a ruler to help you make the 4 boxes.
3. Do you see how the boxes in the chart on page 15 are labeled? Label your chart in the same way.
4. Fill in your chart using information from your book.
   - What interesting facts did you learn?
   - Did the way the book was set up help you understand the facts?
   - Why did you pick this subject?

Sample Nonfiction Chart

Name: Nick López
Date: 3/19/2012

TITLE: *Trees* AUTHOR(S): *Christine Petersen*

MAIN IDEAS
What is this book about? What are the main points and facts? *This book is about trees. Different trees have different kinds of leaves. Trees make seeds.*
INTERESTING FACT
What is the most interesting fact you learned? *Trees are some of the biggest living things.*
BOOK SETUP
How is the book set up? Are there different chapters for different ideas? *There are four parts. Each part is about different ideas.* Is there an index? Does it help you find facts? *Yes. Yes.* Are there pictures? Do they help you understand the subject? *Yes. Yes.*
MY OPINION
Does the book describe the subject in an interesting way? Why or why not? *Yes, because the author asks the reader questions.* Did the book help you learn about the subject? Why or why not? *Yes, because there are many facts. The ideas are easy to understand.* Should others read this book? Why or why not? *Yes, because everyone should learn more about trees.*

CHAPTER FIVE

Writing Your Book Report

Now it is time to write your book report. Take a look at these sample book reports before you begin.

Name: Maria Day
Date: 3/19/2012

Sample Fiction Book Report

I read *Nate the Great and the Hungry Book Club*. The authors are Marjorie Weinman Sharmat and Mitchell Sharmat. The illustrator is Jody Wheeler.

Nate is a detective. His dog, Sludge, is his helper. Nate's friend Rosamond started a book club. There is a problem in this book. One of Rosamond's books has a ripped page. Then the club discovers a page missing in a different book. Who is destroying the books?

Nate visits Rosamond's home. He traces where she's been. He finds clues and solves the mystery.

This is a good book. Nate is funny. I liked trying to figure out the mystery before Nate. You should read this book. Then you can solve the mystery!

Sample Nonfiction Book Report

Name: Nick López
Date: 3/19/2012

Trees is a great book. The author is Christine Petersen.

I enjoyed reading about trees. The most interesting thing I learned was that trees are some of the biggest living things.

The book has four parts. Each part has information about trees. The index helped me find facts. I learned about different kinds of leaves. I also learned that trees make seeds.

The author writes her ideas in fun ways. She compares a tree's roots to long toes! Every other page has a picture. The pictures helped me understand what I read about trees.

This book is a good choice to read in class or for fun. Everyone should learn more about trees!

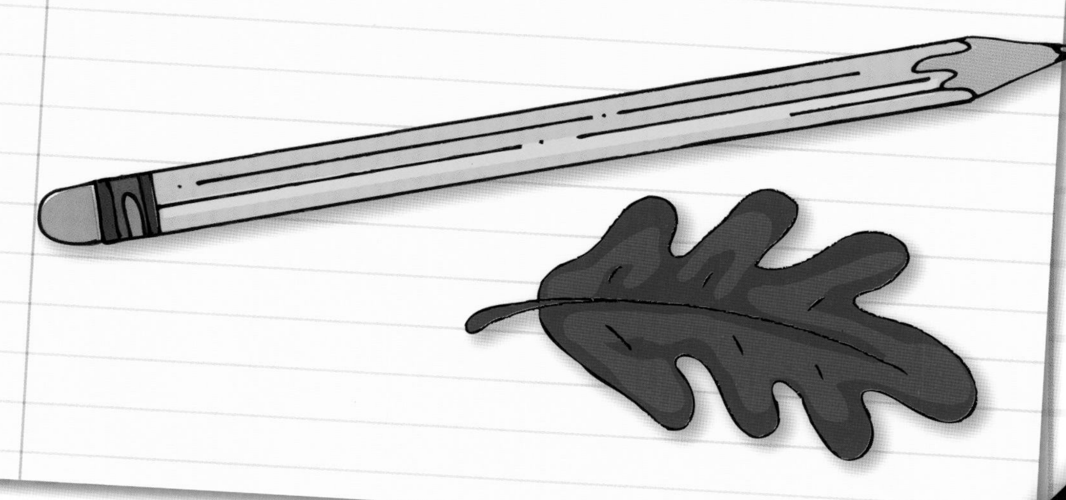

Putting It All Together

Now you are ready to write your book report.

HERE'S WHAT YOU'LL NEED:

- The book
- Your chart
- Notebook paper
- Pen
- Computer (if you want to type the report)

INSTRUCTIONS:

1. Write your name and the date at the top of the paper.
2. Write the title of the book and the name of the author in the first **paragraph** of your report.
3. Use the information in your chart to help you write your report.
4. Use examples or facts from the book to support your ideas.
5. Be sure to **indent** each new paragraph.

Good job! You've written or typed your report. Now you need to check your work.

CHAPTER SIX

Editing

It is important to edit your book report. Read the finished report out loud. This will help you find mistakes. Try it. Does a sentence sound too long? Did you spell the words correctly? Ask an adult to help you. This is the time to make changes to your report.

Try reading your work to a parent. He or she can help you find mistakes.

Checking for Mistakes

Ask yourself these questions as you check your report:

- ☐ YES ☐ NO Did I remember that fiction and nonfiction reports cover different ideas?
- ☐ YES ☐ NO Did I complete the correct chart for the type of book I read?
- ☐ YES ☐ NO Did I use my chart as a guide as I wrote?
- ☐ YES ☐ NO Did I write my name and the date?
- ☐ YES ☐ NO Did I indent my paragraphs?
- ☐ YES ☐ NO Did I leave a space between paragraphs?
- ☐ YES ☐ NO Did I make my ideas clear?
- ☐ YES ☐ NO Did I spell all my words correctly?

Now you know how to write an interesting book report. Which book will you read next?

Glossary

biography (bye-OG-ruh-fee) a person's life story, which is usually written down

characters (KAIR-ik-turz) the people or animals in a story

fiction (FIK-shuhn) writing that tells made-up stories

illustrator (IL-uh-stray-tur) a person who creates pictures for books

indent (in-DENT) to start a line of writing farther in from the left edge of a page than the other lines

index (IN-deks) a list of subjects and the pages where they appear in a book

nonfiction (non-FIK-shuhn) writing that is about real events, people, or things

opinion (uh-PIN-yuhn) a person's beliefs and ideas about somebody or something

paragraphs (PAIR-uh-grafss) groups of sentences about certain ideas or subjects

plot (PLOT) the main story or order of events in a book

setting (SET-ing) the time and place of the action of a story

solution (suh-LOO-shuhn) an explanation of or answer to a problem

For More Information

BOOKS

Faundez, Anne. *How to Write Reports*. Laguna Hills, CA: QEB Publishing, Inc., 2007.

WEB SITES

KidsHealth—How to Pick a Great Book to Read

kidshealth.org/kid/grow/school_stuff/find_book.html

Find out how to choose good books at this site.

TIME for Kids—Book Report

www.timeforkids.com/TFK/kids/hh/writeideas/articles/0,28372,634427,00.html

Look here for tips on writing great book reports.

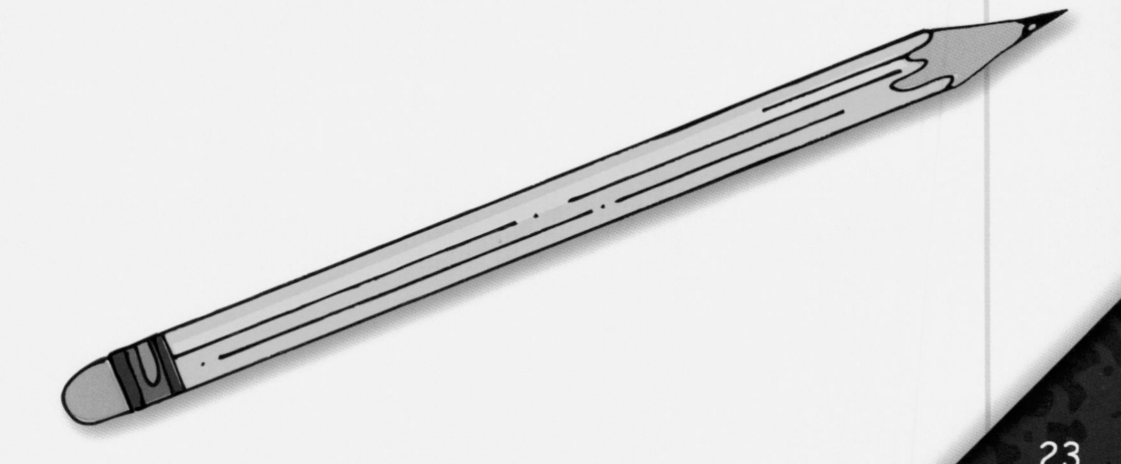

Index

About the Authors

Cecilia Minden, PhD, is the former Director of the Language and Literacy Program at Harvard Graduate School of Education. While at Harvard, Dr. Minden taught several writing courses for teachers. She is now a full-time literacy consultant and the author of more than 100 books for children. Dr. Minden lives in Chapel Hill, North Carolina, with her husband, Dave Cupp, and a cute but spoiled Yorkie named Kenzie.

Kate Roth has a Doctorate from Harvard University in Language and Literacy and a Masters from Columbia University Teachers College in Curriculum and Teaching. Her work focuses on writing instruction in the primary grades. She has taught first grade, kindergarten, and Reading Recovery. She has also instructed hundreds of teachers from around the world in early literacy practices. She lives in Shanghai, China, with her husband and three children, ages 2, 6, and 9. They do a lot of writing to stay in touch with friends and family and record their experiences.